SOPHIE

SOPHIE

❖

Joseph R. Simon

Library of Congress Control Number:		2011918596
ISBN:	Hardcover	978-1-4653-8086-9
	Softcover	978-1-4653-8085-2
	Ebook	978-1-4653-8087-6

This book was printed in the United States of America.

To order additional copies of this book, contact:
Xlibris Corporation
1-888-795-4274
www.Xlibris.com
Orders@Xlibris.com
106889

CONTENTS

DEDICATION

This book is dedicated to my wife Yvonne who stood by me during the writing of the book with compassion and continuous support. Her assistance in finding a place for my mother to live in Florida; the many flights she was required to take in order to resolve the medical issues; the months she stayed with her during her recuperation period; the love she showed for my parents throughout our marriage and her love for me deserves nomination for sainthood.

ACKNOWLEDGEMENTS

First and foremost, I want to thank my mother for maintaining her diary and bringing the pictures with her from Poland to America, which inspired me to write this book. While my first and only intention was to write this story for my children and grandchildren, I showed the manuscript to my neighbor, Violeta Barrett, a published author, and asked her to review the sentence structure and punctuation. She urged me to submit the manuscript to publishers as she felt it should have greater distribution. Thank you VI for your support and assistance. My daughter, Sheryl Motto, a school teacher, also reviewed the text and made numerous revisions to help provide a clear, concise, error-free prose. Thank you for your input. Since I am not a gifted typist I want to thank Sue Ann Fahnenstiel for typing, organizing the script and pictures, and mailing the documents to the publisher. I was so fortunate to have the expertise of Gail Blackhall who provided me with her depth, emotion, and wisdom. My thanks to the staff at Xlibris who guided me through the publishing process with tender loving care. Finally to all my friends and family who encouraged me to publish the memoir, thank you for your eternal optimism, understanding, interest and compassion.

PROLOGUE

This is a story about my mother Sophie, born May 13, 1897 in Poland and died August 21, 2000 in America, the country she called the "Golden Land". It discusses the traumas and hardships experienced during WW 1, as well as her determination and strength needed to recover from the devastation she encountered as she prepared to leave for America. It tells a story how opportunity together with a strong work ethic can change one's life for the better. Her life in America began with a struggle, but as the story continues it proves that sacrifice, perseverance and a positive attitude made a difference in her life. She learned how to enjoy her retirement years and lived a full and happy life. The stories are true as told by her to me and as documented in her writings left to me. The retirement year stories are those that I had the opportunity to personally experience and for which I have fond memories.

The Early Years

The story begins in 1897, in a village in Poland near the Russian border called Gliniany. Sophie was born to Reiselle Bear and Moshe Gutman, the youngest of six children. Her grandfather Hershel Gutman was the owner of a wholesale business that controlled a franchise for the sale of petroleum and salt. These two products were under government control and were distributed by them only to the other businesses in the town. Hershel was a very good politician to receive the franchise and was well-liked and respected in the town. Having the franchise was a great help to their retail business, as vendors placed orders for many of the other items sold in the store when purchasing the petroleum and salt. The store sold sugar, coffee, tea, rice, flour, nuts, herrings, figs, biscuits, wafers, fancy soaps and candles. As a wholesaler, they purchased directly from manufacturers located as far away as Vienna, Austria. Moshe worked for his father as the manager of the retail store.

As the business grew and Hershel aged, Moshe took over as the owner. His younger sister joined in the business as the store manager. Eventually Hershel completely retired from the business, and the entire responsibility fell upon Moshe. The responsibility was more than Moshe could handle. He was ordered by his doctor to slow down and give up smoking. Moshe was a heavy smoker and it was difficult for him to stop, but the scare from his doctor assisted in him doing so. At that time Moshe's wife, Reiselle, stepped in to help in the store. She was very personable and was well liked by everyone she met.

The town where Sophie was born, raised and educated was fairly large with three banks, a number of restaurants and a variety of other retail stores. It was the government center for the surrounding community, with a Village Hall which housed the court and jail. There were no clothing stores as most of the clothes were hand-made by a dressmaker or tailor. Shoes were made by a cobbler and made to order. There were three physicians, two lawyers, one architect and one "Opetheca," a pharmacy.

The "Opetheca" was a showplace with built-in walnut cabinets throughout the store. Each cabinet had a number of drawers that housed the various medicines they made or sold. The pharmacist made most of the prescriptions from scratch, mixing the products together, pounding them on a large mortar board and then weighing them on the special scales hanging on the wall.

The pharmacist was addressed as "Herr Doctor" as he had a doctor's degree, in addition to being a licensed pharmacist. The process was much different from our system of counting the pills and knowing the name of the prescription.

There was also a brewery and a bakery in the town, both of which contributed to the aroma one could detect from the distance. Most homes had ovens in their kitchens, and baked their own breads, cakes and cookies. The bakery specialized in wedding cakes, and special types of breads like holiday challas and crescent rolls.

Sophie didn't remember having a birthday party. She recalled the only celebrations to be when a son was born (a bris) or when there was a wedding. Despite that fact, she indicated that her home was full of joy, with laughter, singing and dancing. She indicated that compared to our lifestyle, it was considered old fashioned as there were no other types of entertainment. She indicated that they were happy and in her infinite wisdom told me: "What you don't have you don't miss".

Even though the household was considered upper class, there was no electricity in their home. Lighting came from kerosene lamps. There was no TV or even a radio. They hadn't been invented yet. The residence was in the back of the building behind the retail store. The building was a brick two-story structure with the store and the family home on the first floor. The second floor had two large apartments which were rented out. Attached to the side of the building was a huge warehouse where the petroleum, salt and other products were stored. The residence consisted of three bedrooms, a dining room, kitchen and a huge pantry. The largest bedroom was for Sophie's parents. The second bedroom was for the three boys and the third bedroom for the three girls. All of the bedrooms were furnished with real hardwood hand carved furniture. The kitchen was huge with a large table and chairs on one side for the morning meal (milkich). On the opposite side, there was another large table and chairs for the noon meal (fleisich). Next to the kitchen, was the dining room with a large oriental rug on the shiny wood floor. There was another large table and chairs in this room. The dining room was only used on Sabbath, holidays or when relatives or other guests were there. The pantry was huge, and also had a shiny wood floor. All of the pots, pans, utensils and groceries were stored there.

They also had animals consisting of two horses and one cow. The animals were kept on a farm outside of town together with their delivery wagon. The farm was located in a large government complex which contained ten, three-story office buildings as well as other farm buildings. It was a restricted area with barbed wire fencing around the entire complex. Sophie stated that it was a well maintained facility which you couldn't see from the main road. It was located a number of miles down a narrow road bordered with different types of blooming trees and flowers. "It smelled like a highly perfumed paradise," said Sophie.

Her family was allowed access to the farm as a result of her family's political affiliation. One of the farm buildings housed the cows, including their cow, in separate stalls. Sophie enjoyed observing milking time, especially when they milked her cow. As a result of owning the cow, they had their own milk, butter and cheese. The farm had a huge vegetable garden, growing all types of vegetables. Their household employee went to the farm twice every day, once to milk their cow and later to pick carrots, potatoes, cabbage, lettuce and tomatoes.

The government school was just eight grades for both boys and girls. The Jewish people didn't send their boys to the government school because there was a picture of Jesus Christ next to the picture of their King in every class. Every morning after singing the national hymn, the class was required to kneel and say a prayer. The Jewish girls didn't have to kneel or say the prayer, but were required to stand silent with their hands clasped together and heads bowed until the prayer was over. The boys were sent to a special private Jewish school organized and supported by a number of philanthropists.

There was also another private Hebrew school for boys and girls sponsored by the Zionist organization. The tuition and money from their fund-raising activities were used to purchase land in Israel. Sophie was impressed that the Zionist organization could have had the vision many years ago to foresee that Israel would eventually become an independent country. The members of the Zionist organization were reformed Jews who smoked on Sabbath and shaved their hair and beards. Sophie's parents were strictly orthodox and she was brought up following the orthodox traditions. The Zionist school was highly accredited. Sophie's friends were enrolled in this facility, and she wanted to go there as well.

She was pleasantly surprised when her parents approved her enrollment. She indicated that those school days were her happiest, as she was with her friends and was able to socialize with the boys in attendance. She told me that she didn't want me to think she was bragging, but she and her five friends received their diplomas in a red velvet cover with a golden star attached for achieving the highest marks in the class. That was quite an achievement since there were over 100 students in her class.

As she pointed out previously, there was no opportunity to go to a higher education facility in her town. In order for her to continue further, she would have to go out of town to a bigger city. All of her friends also wanted to pursue higher education, and decided to find a school they could attend. Because she and her friends had excelled in their previous schooling, they convinced their parents to allow them to register and Sophie's mother allowed her to join them. The schooling was short-lived because at the end of the second year, World War 1 broke out.

Sophie and Friends in Europe

Sophie and Her Classmates

THE WAR

As soon as the news that World War 1 was declared, all of the schools were closed. The banks shut down. Most other businesses, hindered by lack of transportation, did the same. It seemed that everything came to a standstill, and the town became deserted. The young men were called up to serve in the Army, and the men in the Army Reserves were called to active duty. Since Sophie's town was close to the Russian border, the Polish army stationed themselves on the outskirts of town while the Russians were on the opposite side.

The town was in the center of the fighting. Initially, it wasn't too bad as her father had stockpiled a tremendous amount of petroleum and merchandise in their store. They were selling most of the products to the Polish army and receiving cash, which they were able to accumulate and helped them later on. This didn't last very long, as the fighting accelerated with the Russian artillery advancing and bullets flying over their heads. Sophie and her family had to hide in the cellar while this was going on.

As the Russian army came closer, it became obvious that the Polish army couldn't keep them back. All those left in town were told to evacuate. Her grandfather went to the farm to get their horses and wagon. When he returned, Sophie's mother packed the wagon very quickly. In no time, she was sitting in front of the wagon next to Sophie's grandfather. Sophie's mother yelled for the girls to hop in the back of the wagon. Off they went following the Army, who were headed toward the capital city of Lemberg.

This was the city the Russians were aiming for because from there they could advance directly to Warsaw. The shortest way to get there was through Lemberg. That was why the village of Gliniany was hit so badly. Her grandfather and mother tried hard to follow the Army, but were having trouble keeping up the pace. They wanted to get to Lemberg before the Russians arrived there. When they finally did arrive, they considered themselves fortunate. Her mother was so happy that she had accumulated and saved the cash she had with her. She was able to find an apartment to rent, hoping that the family wouldn't have to stay too long. She was scared that the money would eventually run out, and she wouldn't know where to go to be safe until the war was over.

Fortunately the capital city of Lemberg is located on top of the highest mountain, and was surrounded by other high peaks. It was a fortress within the mountain protected on all sides. When the Russians reached the outskirts of the city, they were unable to climb the mountain with their artillery forces. They also were not able to see where the Polish army was located.

The Polish armies had the tactical advantage and were bombarding the Russians. The Russian army was incurring multiple casualties, but they refused to give up and continued to fight vigorously. The Russians needed to capture Lemberg, so that they could go on to Warsaw. The Polish army continued its assault punishing the Russians further, and wouldn't give them a chance to move ahead or forward.

As soon as the Russians tried to move, the Polish army kept hitting harder without mercy and continued the slaughter. Finally, the Russians realized that it was futile to stay there without gaining any territory and losing more men. They decided to retreat and go home. This phase of the war was over with the Polish army victorious. A couple of weeks later, everyone was told that they could go back to their homes. They were excited to hear the news, not realizing what was waiting for them when they returned.

After the War

When Sophie's family arrived home, they were shocked to see the huge damage. Only tall brick walls remained, no roofs, windows, or doors, and all of their personal property was missing or damaged. They were numb. While standing there looking at the empty walls, tears were running down their faces. They couldn't believe what they were seeing and what was left of their home. They were heart-broken and found it difficult to face or accept. While they were standing there motionless, in shock, a neighbor came running to them. She told Sophie's mother that there was a house outside of the village available for rent. Her mother rushed to see the place and decided to rent it. When the family arrived, they realized it was not much of a home as compared to their old home. Since there was no other option, they had to be grateful and would adjust. Everyone helped to unload the wagon and bring what little belongings they had into the house. That was the beginning of their struggle and hardship trying to get settled in a home much smaller and with minimal furnishings.

Sophie's older sister was a delicate and frail person and wasn't able to cope with the change. She got sick, caught pneumonia and died. This was a terrible shock to her mother, who was having difficulty understanding why this was happening. The family sat shiva to grieve and remember her sister. At the end of the week, her mother went to see the funeral director to pay the funeral expenses. She still was full of grief. While there, she collapsed and died instantly. She apparently had been stricken with a fatal heart attack.

Sophie could not come up with words to describe how she felt, and had a difficult time dealing with this double tragedy. It was bad enough coming home to see the destruction of her family's residence which her father and grandfather had worked so hard to establish, but the loss of her sister and mother was too much for her to bear. She said it left a big scar in her heart.

"Wars are inhuman and barbaric," she said. Without her mother and in this new environment, for Sophie her home was no home anymore. Her father finally came back from the army and told her that one of her brothers was killed in action and her other two brothers left to work with relatives that lived in Lemberg. The only ones remaining there were her father, older sister and herself.

Sophie decided it was time to leave too and went to visit her mother's oldest sister who also lived in Lemberg. They were fortunate that they had very little damage to their home from the war. They were glad to have Sophie stay there, but her older sister who stayed home got lonely and asked Sophie to come back home. She left to be with her sister, but when she got there she wasn't happy because nothing had changed. It was still no longer a home.

All of her friends had left for America so she wanted to leave too, but had no way of getting there. She decided to visit her uncle, her mother's youngest brother, who lived in Krackow. While there, her uncle received a letter from his youngest sister from Germany. When she heard that Sophie was there, she invited her to come to Germany. Sophie did not know that she had an aunt in Germany. Sophie wrote her aunt and told her she would be happy to visit and asked for information on how to get there. Her aunt answered her letter and gave her the directions.

Sophie didn't waste any time to do the paperwork necessary to apply for a travel visa. She was anxious to meet her aunt who had told Sophie she would help her. This turned out to be one trip she wished she had never made. It would have been better if she had never met her new-found aunt.

THE TRIP

She began her trip to Germany on an early Friday morning on a special speedy nonstop express train. Her first stop was to be Chenstochow where her aunt and uncle were supposed to meet her. The train was speeding along and when she felt the train was slowing down she knew she was getting close to her stop. The train came to a halt and when she heard the conductor mumble something that sounded like Chenstochow she picked up her suitcase and got off. As soon as she got off the train it took off like lightening and there she was the only person to get off at this place that was supposed to be a station. She looked around and realized there was no station, no buildings, no houses and she was all alone. It was nothing but a wilderness with visible destruction resulting from the war.

Her aunt and uncle were not there to meet her and she had no way to contact them. She said she took a deep breath, trying not to panic, thinking that they were delayed or that something must have happened to them to cause the delay. She paced back and forth looking out of the corners of her eyes anxiously hoping that they would show up. She couldn't understand why they told her to get off in this desolate place and why they were not there. As she looked around she realized she was in the middle of an old battle zone. The grass had grown high and it had turned into a wilderness.

Suddenly, out of the blue, she saw a young boy running down the hill, heading toward her. She guessed he was around 12 years old. When he was next to her he asked: "Do want a hotel?" "Where?", she asked. "Right here up the hill," he said. Sophie had no other choice so she let him pick up her suitcase and followed him to the hotel. As they got to the top of the hill she saw a big sign that said "HOTEL" and nothing else.

When they got there the boy put down her suitcase and ran away. She had no other choice but to pick up her suitcase and continued to walk until she saw a building with a hotel sign above the door. When she opened the door all she saw was a big frame on all sides with a roof above. She became nervous and began to run with her suitcase back down the hill. She ran until she was completely exhausted and couldn't go any further. She put her suitcase on the ground and sat on it to rest.

She said that she began to pray for some miracle to happen. While she was deeply in prayer she said a flash came over her face. She said she looked up and saw her mother's face and heard something inside of her saying, "Run, Run, Run." She picked up her suitcase and began to run. For a while she saw nothing but wilderness but eventually she saw a light in the distance. As she approached she saw a highway and a number of business places. She finally reached one of the stores and after she entered she collapsed on the floor. She said she didn't remember anything that happened and while she was lying on the floor she raised her head and saw a couple staring at her. She said she was bewildered and kept turning her head, looking at them. She didn't know what was going on.

As she stared at the couple, the woman stretched out her hand and asked: "Where do you come from and who are you?" When Sophie heard her soft motherly voice she came to and started to talk. She then began to realize what happened to her and told the couple the story that her aunt and uncle were supposed to meet her there. She also told them about the boy who took her to the hotel and how she ran away. The woman responded that she was a lucky girl and very smart. Apparently Sophie had run away from a slaughter house. She explained to Sophie that if anyone got stranded there this young boy would come running down and lead them to this "make believe" hotel. He then would run off and call a gangster group and tell them that he brought someone to the hotel. He got paid by them for his efforts. The woman said that a number of people had been killed there.

Sophie asked the woman if there was a hotel in town that she could go to and call her aunt to tell her where she was. The woman responded by telling her that there was nothing left standing, that Hitler had killed all the Jews where the hotel was located. The Russians had fought against the Germans at this location and when the Russians retreated the Germans burned all the buildings and left this wilderness. The store that they were in was one of the first buildings to be rebuilt and the town was beginning to be restored. The woman told Sophie to leave her suitcase there and come with her. She had just completed her grocery shopping and said the delivery boy would bring the groceries and suitcase to her house. The woman lived a half block away from the store and took Sophie home with her.

RESCUED

Sophie walked with the woman to her home and became very talkative. She told her who her relatives were. When the woman heard the name "Gronwitter," she said she knew who they were. She told Sophie that as soon as they got to her house she would call them. She told Sophie that she could stay at her place until her relatives came for her. When they got to her home, Sophie was surprised to see the dining room table covered with a linen tablecloth, candles in a candle holder, and a white embroidered napkin holder which would hold a challah. She was so relieved that she was in a home comparable to that of her parent's home.

She was completely exhausted and asked the woman if she could sit down. She thanked her for her kindness and told her she didn't know how she could repay her. The woman told Sophie that she was going to make a cup of tea for her. She said that as soon as the groceries arrived, she was going to get dinner ready and light the candles. When the tea was ready, Sophie said that she was so exhausted and wasn't up to drinking it. She apologized to the woman, and told her she was sorry but she didn't feel she could drink or eat anything. She really needed to rest. The woman helped her to the couch, where she took off her shoes and laid down. Sophie fell asleep immediately and didn't awake until the next day.

When she did the woman asked her how she felt. She told Sophie that she was a very sick girl, and that she had stayed up with her during the night. She told Sophie that her pulse was low and that sweat was dripping from her body. She kept changing the wet towels very carefully, so as not to awaken her. She was a nurse and knew how important it was for Sophie to rest. She told her that her pulse was so low that she was afraid that she would catch pneumonia. She said she was worried about her, and was thankful that she was feeling better. She urged

Sophie to go shower, freshen up and change her clothes, and that when she returned breakfast would be waiting for her.

When Sophie came down for breakfast she asked if she could call her aunt and tell her where she was. The woman said that she had already done that, and that she had given her aunt a piece of her mind. She asked the aunt how she could have done such a horrible thing, leaving this young girl stranded and not showing up. Her aunt told the woman that she was sorry and apologized. Her aunt explained that her husband had a bad day in the stock market and wasn't able to go with her. She was afraid to go by herself. Her aunt told the woman that she was sending a car to pick her up and get her through the border in order to bring Sophie to her house. Sophie said that the trip to visit her aunt was more than she expected or needed. She thanked the woman for her hospitality and told her she hoped she would be able to reciprocate her kindness some day.

When Sophie arrived at her aunt's house, she couldn't look directly at her and told her she was not staying. She said she didn't want to listen to their lame excuses and wanted to go home. The next day her aunt took her to the Registration Bureau to fill out papers and got her a return ticket home. She went home on the same speedy express train straight to Lemberg.

When Sophie got home, it was no better than it was when she left. Her friends were no longer there. They had gone to America. She said there was not much left there for her. Her mother and older sister were dead, one brother was killed in the war, and the other two brothers were in different towns. She didn't know what happened to her father or her sister. She only knew that she was desperate to find a way to get to America.

To America

Sophie was close to her 18th birthday and was getting tired and frustrated running back and forth to her relatives. She really wanted to go to America and join up with her friends and family. She recalled that she had an uncle in America who was married to her mother's sister who she never met.

She remembered her mother telling her how she helped her uncle when his wife became ill. She had brought them to her home, and had cared for her until she passed away. After her death, her uncle no longer wanted to remain in Europe and immigrated to America. At that time, he wasn't able to take all his family with him and left two young boys with her mother until he could bring them to America. Her mother took care of the boys for a number of months until her brother-in-law was able to call for them.

Sophie decided to write to her uncle and ask him if he could help her get to America. When she received his reply, she was thrilled to read that he was willing to do everything he could to help her. He said that he would apply for a visa for her and complete the necessary paperwork. He told Sophie that he would send her a ticket as soon as the papers were completed.

When Sophie received the ticket, she went to the Immigration Bureau to request permission to leave. She was advised by them that travel to America had tightened and the Bureau had placed a quota. They were restricting the number of people they were allowing to leave each year. They had also established a preferential order as additional criteria. The order was:

(1) European children with parents in America;
(2) European wives with husbands in America;

(3) European sisters or brothers with sisters or brothers in America;
(4) Other family relationships.

She realized that it would take some time before her number would come up. She was determined to stay the course, even though she said there were times that she almost gave up. It was tough luck for a teenager to have had to experience.

Finally, she was notified to go to Warsaw to sign the papers and receive her visa to leave for America. When the visa arrived, she took a train from Warsaw to Rotterdam. There she boarded a huge Cunard Liner and sailed for America.

While sailing, she was able to send correspondence to all her friends and her uncle. When she arrived at Ellis Island and saw the Statue of Liberty, she began to cry. They were tears of happiness. She was also thrilled to meet her uncle who was there to greet her. The following day, she called her friends who were glad to hear that she was in New York. They told her they would come to meet her at her uncle's house after they got out off work.

In America

Sophie's friends arrived at her uncle's house with presents for her. She said it was a joyous event with everyone laughing and crying happily. They told her about their lives in New York, including where they were working. All five told her that they would help her find a job and would keep in constant touch with her. As a matter of fact, one of her friends called two days later and advised that she had a friend who was the head lady at a hat factory. She had told her about Sophie and the suffering she had gone through to get to New York. She then told Sophie to contact her because there were openings at the factory.

Two of her friends went with Sophie to meet the lady at the factory. They wanted to be with her, as they knew Sophie's English was not perfect. Even though all of them had taken English language courses in Europe, she hadn't spoken English in a conversation. The lady at the factory took a liking to Sophie and hired her immediately. Sophie told her that her language skills were better in Polish, German, Russian and Hebrew, but she would work to improve her English. The factory lady told Sophie that she was most interested in her sewing skills and everything else would fall into place.

Sophie began working the next day. Her uncle was so happy and relieved that Sophie had found a job so quickly. He offered to drive her to and from work. Sophie liked her job, which was to sew flowers on the crowns of hats. What she didn't know was that the hat business had only two short seasons, spring and fall. The factory was closed during the summer and winter months. By the end of May, the job was finished so she had to look for another job. Because she had only been in America for four months and spoke broken English, it wasn't that easy for her to find work.

Her uncle had a cousin who owned a hotel in the Catskill Mountains. When he spoke with his cousin, she told him to have Sophie come see her. Sophie took a bus and went to the mountains to meet with her cousin, who was surprised to see that Sophie was only a teenager. They spent the evening talking about family and the traumas Sophie experienced while she was growing up. She told Sophie it was hot in New York City in the summer, but cool in the mountains. She would find something for her to do at the hotel. If she liked working at the hotel, she could stay there or if she wanted to go back to the city in the fall that would okay with her.

Sophie decided to stay at the hotel for the summer and worked at various jobs. Initially, she worked in housekeeping, but eventually ended up in the dining room. She was proficient in all of the jobs she performed. At first she was a bus girl cleaning tables and dishes. Later on she was elevated to a waitress.

While she was a waitress, she was fortunate to meet a young single man who ate dinners each evening at the hotel. His name was Jacob and was 23 years old. He was also brought to America when he was 18 years old. His uncle, Frank Honigsbaum owned the department store in the town. Jacob lived with his uncle and aunt in an apartment above the store. Sophie and Jacob had a lot in common in terms of their experiences in Europe and their migration to America. They enjoyed talking to each other and spent a lot of time together during the summer.

Jacob told Sophie that upon arrival in America his uncle, Frank, suggested that he enlist in the Army. His uncle was concerned, that since he was not a citizen, he might get drafted and be placed on the front line in the infantry. When the war ended, Jacob received an honorable discharge with citizenship papers.

Sophie told Jacob that she was going back to the city, and hoped that they could write each other and keep in touch. Jacob agreed to communicate with her and was pleased that she wanted to continue the relationship.

In September, Sophie went back to the city and began to look for a new job. She was speaking better English by now and was able to read the advertisements. Fortunately, she was able to find a job in a dress factory earning $45.00 a week. Sophie worked in the dress industry for four years. She continued to communicate with Jacob by mail during the four years she was working in the city, until the day he asked her to come back to the mountains to spend the rest of her life with him.

[I asked Sophie if she had gone to see Jacob during the four years she was working in the city and was surprised to learn that she hadn't. It seemed strange to me that two people could make arrangements to marry without seeing each other. I mentioned that to Sophie and her response was that I never saw or read the letters that they wrote.]

Sophie and Her Friends in the Catskills

Sophie in the Catskills

TANNERSVILLE

Sophie went back to the Catskill Mountains to marry Jacob Simon, and live in a small village called Tannersville. Jacob was working as the general manager of his uncle's department store. After they were married, the couple lived in a small apartment on the fourth floor of the building. Prior to marrying Sophie, Jacob liked to spend his spare time riding his motor bike over the back roads and mountain trails. Sophie convinced him to sell the bike and purchase an automobile in its place. She was concerned for his safety, and also wanted to spend their spare time together. She was not going to ride on the motor bike with him, and said a car would be more preferable. He bought a new 1929 Chevrolet Coupe. As a result, they spent many of their weekends riding though the small mountain towns. She said that they enjoyed meeting up with other couples who were fortunate to own a car, joining them at lakes and parks for picnics. It was fortunate that they traveled in groups, as there was a major imperfection in the vehicles that surfaced quite frequently. Many of the roads that they traveled on were made of dirt or stone, which strained the axles on their cars. Sophie said they broke an axle once a month. The other cars in the caravan would tow them home, and then to the garage for repair. She said she got tired of this practice, and convinced the other couples to picnic around the lake in town.

Sophie joined a Hadassah group, and was actively involved with them. However, this activity was not enough for her to do, as she soon got bored with staying home. She then registered herself in adult education courses with the ultimate goal of getting a high school diploma. This was short-lived as the stock market crashed and the great depression followed. Business slowed down and people moved out of town to find employment. It wasn't long before many businesses were boarded up and stores were for sale.

Jacob's uncle also decided to close his store and move to the state capital in Albany to open another store. They asked Jacob to go with them to be the manager in the new store. He and Sophie decided to stay in town, and see if they could buy one of the vacant stores to start their own business. The majority of the stores that closed had mortgages that had defaulted. The mortgages were mostly held by one individual named Paul Fromer.

He was an influential lawyer, banker and the sole owner of the utility company. In his role as president of the bank, he approved the business loans and personally guaranteed them. When the business people left town and defaulted on their loans, Paul took title to the properties and became the owner. Jacob and Paul were good friends and active members of the local American Legion chapter. Sophie convinced Jacob to ask Paul if they could buy one of the closed businesses he owned. There was only one problem. "Money!" Paul was thrilled to unload one of the properties, and said he would sell it for $10,000 with no down payment and take back a 20 year mortgage with interest at 1%. That was a real bargain, and something Sophie and Jacob could afford. They were the first to purchase one of the many closed stores Paul owned.

The building was a two story structure with an apartment above the store. There was a porch in the front of the building, extending out from the apartment section. The building had been well maintained and required little if any repair. They opened their own dry goods store, naming it Simon's Department Store. Sophie said it was difficult at first because they didn't have much money to buy merchandise. Fortunately, Jacob knew many of the wholesalers, distributors and sales representatives from his former position at his uncle's store.

Without Jacob's knowledge, Sophie went to see Paul at the bank and applied for a loan to buy merchandise. She told him she would leave her diamond engagement ring as collateral. Sophie said he told her that the ring wouldn't fit him and he had enough problems unloading the buildings he owned. He didn't want to deal in jewelry. He told her to keep her ring, go buy the merchandise they needed, and when the bills came due he would open a line of credit for them to pay the invoices. He trusted Sophie and Jacob and never asked them to sign any papers, shook Sophie's hand and wished her good luck. [Sounds incredible doesn't it?] Sophie didn't tell Jacob about the arrangement she had with Paul, but urged him to begin ordering merchandise. He was not comfortable buying merchandise without having the money to cover the bills. She told him she would contact the companies and sign contracts with them to get the merchandise on consignment. Needless to say, she never did that, but it allowed Jacob to feel comfortable ordering merchandise.

The merchandise was ordered from well-known companies that most customers knew were quality products. Many residents of the town wanted those products but couldn't afford the price. Sophie was an excellent sales person and convinced them to purchase the products by paying what they could and charge the difference. Jacob wasn't comfortable with that arrangement, but once it started he had no other choice but to live with it. Sophie got tired of listening to Jacob's pessimism. She was a risk taker and full of confidence. From that time forward, Jacob was assigned the responsibility of keeping the store neat and clean, while Sophie was the buyer, sales guru and the financial wheeler dealer. The arrangements Sophie made worked out well, as the customers paid the balances they owed and Sophie paid Paul the money to cover the line of credit.

During the Depression years, Sophie was very charitable and she gave merchandise to church groups for them to raise money. She also gave free merchandise to many of the poor families in town, as she wanted them to feel comfortable and look good at graduations or other special events they were attending. She would shake their hands and wish them good luck. I think this was her way to pay back for some of the favors and kindnesses she had received while growing up.

It took three years for the economy to turn around, and the Catskills were booming again. In the summer, camps opened, hotels and motels were built and homes were being constructed overlooking the mountain cliffs. These houses were built by wealthy and famous people who had homes and businesses in New York City. The mountains were only a three hour drive, so the wives and children stayed for the summer and the fathers came for the weekend. The houses were built in private gated communities with restricted access. Two residents of note were the actress, Maude Adams, the first American to play the role of Peter

Pan and the banker, Edward Coleman Delafield, President of Bank of America. Many of these people owned racing horses which they housed and raced at a flat track in Saratoga an hour away.

The racing season was for three weeks in August, and the race track was nationally known. After the races, when their horses won and they made money on their bets, these customers spent a lot of money in the store. Sophie allowed these people to have charge privileges even though Jacob had a large sign made, which was prominently displayed, saying: "No Charge Accounts." Jacob would look at her in amazement when she did this, but she just smiled and sold a lot of merchandise.

The Delafields had a number of children, and the kids often came with their Nanny in a chauffeured limousine to buy much of their play clothes and sneakers. They had one of the largest charge balances, which Sophie allowed them to maintain throughout the summer while making Jacob nervous. Before their family left to go back to New York City, they would pay up in full. Sophie would look at Jacob and smile.

The fall season brought visitors to view the falling leaves and changing colors of the trees. Many of the locals tapped the trees for maple syrup, and sold their products on roadside stands. The woods were full of deer, and the mountains had black bears wandering around. The hunting season lasted for about three weeks in the fall. It really wasn't safe in the woods, as many of the city folk were loose cannons.

Business was good in the store, as the hunters never brought the appropriate clothes with them. Two major ski trails were built in the mountains and the winter weekends were full with skiers. Business was growing so fast that Sophie had to get sales help to assist them. Big box stores like K Mart were being built in towns below the mountains, and Sophie and Jacob were concerned that they would take business away from them. Amazingly, the locals continued to patronize their store, as they considered them family and were thankful for what Sophie had done for them during the Depression years.

In the fall of 1934, Sophie became pregnant and guess who arrived on the scene in June 1935. "ME." This was the second time she attempted motherhood, as she previously had a miscarriage two years earlier. She was now 38 years old and needed help to take care of her newborn infant, as she spent most of her time in the store. She was fortunate to find a wonderful woman to assist, who continued to help in raising me until I was school age.

As I grew up, our household was full of laughs and interesting stories. The happiest day occurred on November 15, 1937 when Mother received her citizenship papers. She told me that this was the moment she came alive, as her second dream came true. I didn't have to ask what the first dream was; as I knew it was me.

During my childhood years, Mother tried to balance her time between working in the store and being with me. In the winter, I recall her climbing hills and snow banks while we both were on snowshoes. When I began to downhill ski, I saw pictures of her on skis trying to show me that she could do it too. Fortunately the pictures were taken in our backyard on flat ground. We even got my father to participate by putting on snowshoes.

Mother came to every school event I participated in. She didn't particularly like watching my football games, as she was worried that I might get hurt. She enjoyed watching basketball and baseball, and was thrilled that I was involved with sports. Fortunately, I only had minor injuries from these activities. I also played trombone in the school band. She really loved watching me during parades, dressed in our colorful uniforms, and reminding everyone to look for me in the first row. She thought I was there because of my talent, but I advised her that was not true because trombones were always in the front row.

Since my mother spent most of her time in the store, she would sneak upstairs when business was slow to be with me and to cook the meals. Our main meal was dinner, and my mother cooked everything in her pressure cooker. She would leave the cooker on the stove and go back down to the store. It seems that she always got involved with customers and forgot about the food. If the pot was left too long on the burner, the top would release and shoot up through the ceiling. It was comparable to watching a mini launch. The handyman who my father used to patch the ceiling had an annuity as this was a regular occurrence.

The next fiasco came when my father wanted to make it easier for my mother to do laundry, and bought her a huge state of the art appliance that both washed and dried clothes in the same unit. It was so complicated to work that my mother never used it. She would wash clothes by hand and hang everything on a clothes line. She said clothes got cleaner by hand wash, and she liked the fresh smell of drying outside. My father went ballistic that she wouldn't use the machine. To pacify him, she threw his underwear in the machine and turned it on. The machine jammed, burnt the motor out and ruined my father's clothes. My father then traded it in for an automatic washer, which my mother used occasionally. The good news was that the unit took less space than the other monster.

My mother was an exceptional baker. Her apple pie and bread rolls were to die for. But her cooking skills left a lot to be desired, as everything she cooked was well done. She was slicing her roast with her electric knife. It was falling apart by itself, but we told her it would work better if she plugged it in.

My father loved to acquire any new product that came on the market. We had the first TV on the mountain top. It was either a 5 or 7 inch black and white unit. The only problem was that it was difficult to get reception because of the mountain range. The solution was to erect a high antenna on the roof, and of course my father wanted it to rotate so we could get as many channels that were available. We were able to get reception after that. The next problem was that when there were heavy winds, the antenna hummed loudly, which drove my mother crazy. When there were strong rainstorms, we always cringed and were scared that it would end up acting like a lightening rod. I imagine the antenna cost much more than the TV, but the good news is that it lasted for the entire time they lived there and worked well with all of the TV's purchased later.

My parents retired in 1975, and sold their business to a young couple who grew up in town. At that time, I was a partner in the international accounting firm of Coopers and Lybrand and arranged, as part of the sale and purchase agreement, to allow my parents to live in their apartment until they no longer wanted to, by paying rent to the young couple. This worked out well, until my father died on Christmas day in

1979. My mother no longer wanted to stay there. We invited her to come live with us in Albany until she knew what she wanted to do. She told us she was tired of cold weather, didn't want to inconvenience us, and said Florida is where she wanted to go. Thus, the 40 years spent in Tannersville came to an end.

During the time the above mentioned events occurred, I married Yvonne and we had three children. Yvonne and I try to go back to Tannersville on an annual basis to visit my parents' grave sites. We always stop in town for lunch, and it is amazing that the stores are now owned by third and fourth generation children of families that I knew. My parents' store is now a Mexican restaurant. We went for lunch there. When I introduced myself to the owner and told him that I grew up in his building, we had a lovely conversation. He asked if I had pictures of my parents' store that I could send him. I told him that I did. When we got back home, I went through my mother's album and sent them to him. He responded with a nice note thanking me, and told me that the next time we come to town the lunch was on him.

Obviously, the village has changed a lot since I grew up there. Tannersville has again experienced a revival in the 21st century. This can be attributed largely to the efforts of a historic foundation who implemented the town wide Paint Program, which was the vision of Elena Patterson, a local artist. With the help and support of corporate sponsors and the local residents, the Paint Project Program was implemented. The project involved painting the store fronts in multicolored pastels, often with cartoon-like pictures on the shutters. It has attracted waves of tourists who come to see the dramatic paint schemes, and continue to annoy local residents who have been quoted saying; "They look ridiculous." The project prompted much attention when it was publicized in the New York Times magazine section. The project was also featured on NBC's show "Today," on CNBC and on all three of the local Albany-based networks. The Tannersville Main Street Historic District has now been listed on the National Register of Historic Places.

Sophie and Jacob's Honeymoon

Miss Sophie Gutman
Mr. Jacob Simon
Married

At Home
Tannersville,
Green County
February 15th, 1931   New York

Wedding Announcement

Wedding Portraits of Jacob and Sophie

Jacob and His Cycle

Sophie and Jacob at Picnics

Simon's Department Store

Sophie's Favorite

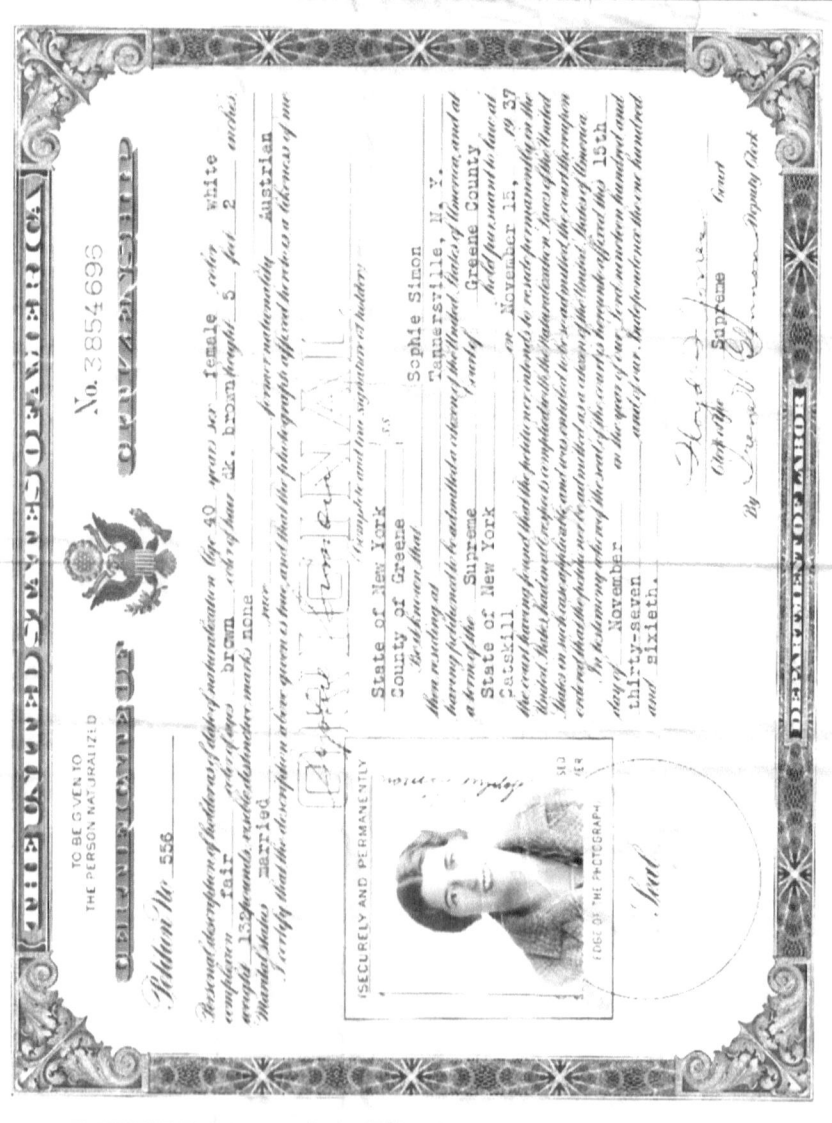

THE UNITED STATES OF AMERICA

No. 3854695

TO BE GIVEN TO
THE PERSON NATURALIZED

CERTIFICATE OF CITIZENSHIP

Petition No. 556

Personal description of holder as of date of naturalization: Age 40 years; sex female; color white; complexion fair; color of eyes brown; color of hair dk. brown; height 5 feet 2 inches; weight 135 pounds; visible distinctive marks none; from her nationality Austrian; Marital status married; former nationality

I certify that the description above given is true, and that the photograph affixed hereto is a likeness of me.

Sophie Simon

ORIGINAL
(Complete and true signature of holder)

State of New York
County of Greene } ss

Be it known that Sophie Simon
Tannersville, N. Y.
then residing at
having petitioned to be admitted a citizen of the United States of America, and at
a term of the Supreme Court of Greene County
State of New York held pursuant to law at
Catskill on November 15, 1937
the court having found that the petitioner intends to reside permanently in the United States (when so required by the naturalization laws of the United States), had in all other respects complied with the applicable provisions of the naturalization laws of the United States, and was entitled to be so admitted, the court thereupon ordered that the petitioner be and (s)he was admitted as a citizen of the United States of America.

In testimony whereof the seal of the court is hereunto affixed this 15th
day of November in the year of our Lord nineteen hundred and
thirty-seven and of our Independence the one hundred
and sixtieth.

Floyd _____
Christopher _____ Supreme Court
By Clerk _____ Deputy Clerk

[SECURELY AND PERMANENTLY]
EDGE OF THE PHOTOGRAPH

[Seal]

DEPARTMENT OF LABOR

Citizenship Papers

Tannersville Store Front
Photo by Upstater

Pancho Villa Mexican Restaurant

Winter Scenes and Band Picture

Pre-Florida

Before I continue to discuss my Mother's move to Florida, I feel it appropriate to provide some background information on how my mother and my wife, Yvonne became so close. For many years, after we were married, Yvonne and I would visit and help my parents in the store, mostly on Holiday weekends such as Fourth of July, Memorial Day, Labor Day, Thanksgiving and Christmas. We continued to do this even after our children were born.

Behind the store there was a small creek and the kids loved wading in the water fishing for minnows. During their younger years, they would ride their tricycles throughout the store under the dress racks and drive my father crazy. We never allowed them to ride outside the store, as it was located on the main street and would be dangerous. As they got older, they loved going to visit their grandparents and began assisting and helping in the store. The best part was that they never went home without new sneakers and other clothes.

Next door to my parents' store was a restaurant. Our kids would go in on their own and order ice cream cones or sodas. When it became time to pay, they told the owner their names and said that I would come in later to pay. This became a regular occurrence. Before long, they expanded their purchases to include candy and food. They would then sit on high-top stools, barely able to reach the counter, and talk to the owner. He enjoyed listening to the stories they told about their home life, especially about me. He would relate stories about me to them; covering the time I lived and grew up there.

Sophie especially like our visits, as the help in the store was greatly appreciated. More importantly, on Thanksgiving and Christmas the store was closed, and she enjoyed sitting around the dining room table telling and listening to stories.

I was an only child. From the time I dated Yvonne, my mother adored her. After we got married, she considered her as if she was her daughter. They both had experienced traumas and hardships as children. Yvonne told my Mother about her childhood. As each related and compared their life experiences, their bond became much tighter. Rather than for me to describe what Yvonne went through I am including an article she wrote in our Homeowners' newspaper, entitled "I Remember When".

I Remember When

In memory of both of my parents by Yvonne Simon

I REMEMBER when this picture was taken in 1948. With the urging and assistance of my Aunt living in America my family and I had migrated to this country from Amsterdam Holland. My brother and I were placed in a Michigan school classroom, immediately, without knowing one word of English. One of the first things we learned was to recite the American Flag salute in English. The 3rd child from the left is me and next to me is my brother.

Before we came to the United States I remember receiving packages from my Aunt in America with all kinds of goodies. I REMEMBER eating green and red jello. We were so fascinated by the jiggily stuff. We never saw anything like it before.

My brother and I were born in Bangdung Indonesia. My father was Dutch and my mother was Hungarian. Life was good in Indonesia for us before the war broke out. And then all of a sudden the war started and the Country was invaded and occupied by the Japanese. Dad had to go fight as a soldier in the Dutch army and all Dutch women and children were placed into concentration camps. My mother was only 25 years old at the time and had to take care, not only of 2 small children, but also my grandmother and sick Aunt. We were in the concentration camp for 4 years. I was there from the age of 4-8 and unfortunately still have some vivid memories. I REMEMBER hiding and crawling under beds and shelters when the Japanese bombed areas near where we were.

I REMEMBER eating only small bowls of rice and eating every morsel until there was no more.

I REMEMBER my mother taking care of us when an epidemic spread throughout the camp and everyone got sick.

I REMEMBER walking in the hot sun for hours as a punishment and seeing older people collapsing from the heat.

I REMEMBER my mother being slapped across her face by a Japanese soldier. During those 4 years we never received any correspondence nor did we know whether our father was still alive.

Thank g-d when the war was over, with the help of the American Red Cross, my Dad was able to find us. He decided to take our family to Holland, where he grew up, to hopefully find other members of his family alive.

I REMEMBER when we first arrived in Holland asking what the white stuff was on the ground. Was it sugar? No, Dad told me, that white stuff was called snow. Indonesia weather was just like Florida—always hot.

SOPHIE

We lived in Holland for two years and then came to America and lived in Michigan for six months. We then moved to Binghamton where my Father found a job with the same company that he worked for in Holland. I grew up in Binghamton, New York and lived there until I went to college in Syracuse.

I REMEMBER that it was a long hard struggle for my parents since they had lost everything they had as a result of the war. However, as I look back, I can't recall being an unhappy child. We always had the love and understanding by two wonderful parents. We never had many luxuries as children, but never felt deprived.

I thank G-d for what I have today. A wonderful loving and ambitious husband, three healthy married children and seven grandchildren that I am very proud of.

I just recently lost my mother at age 93 and that's when I found this picture at her house when we cleaned up. It brought back many memories and therefore motivated me to write this article as we approach the Holiday season.

Wishing all of you a very Healthy and Happy New Year.

Yvonne Simon

FLORIDA

In August 1980, my wife Yvonne took my mother to Florida to help her find a place to live. They went to Ft. Lauderdale, as we had a friend who was a real estate agent there. They looked everywhere, but my mother was getting cold feet for the first time in her life. Yvonne found a perfect spot for her in a condominium complex called Polynesian Gardens. It was located in Plantation, and consisted of five high-rise apartment buildings with all types of activity centers. There was an Olympic size pool, a two lane bowling alley, shuffleboard courts, two tennis courts and a theatre building where they had shows, movies, bingo and other social activities. Most importantly, it was located within walking distance of a strip mall which included a large grocery store and other small stores. The only problem was that there were no available units for sale. Yvonne was really disappointed.

After they came home, we received a call from the agent that the model apartment on the first floor of building five was available. It was a turn-key arrangement, fully furnished and decorated for $50,000. I was so excited to hear this as the market in Florida was really hot. I asked our agent to immediately put down a deposit to hold the property, take pictures, and send me the contract and pictures by overnight mail. This was when the fun and games began. We showed the pictures to mother and told her this was perfect for her. I told her she would have to pay cash for the property, as I doubted any bank would give an eighty-two year old a mortgage. She was hesitant to go that route, as she was afraid that she wouldn't have enough money left to live on. I didn't want to lose this opportunity, so I told my mother that I would purchase the apartment for her and she could pay rent to me. The rent I would charge would be the amount I would need to cover the debt service and other expenses. After hemming and hawing, she agreed to that arrangement. We went to Florida with mother to finalize the deal and get her settled.

It didn't take long for my mother to meet people and make friends. They would sit around the pool and chat about everything, mostly about their families and their former lives. My mother liked doing this and in no time became one of the "girls", as she called them. It didn't take long for the conversation to discuss her arrangement with me, and that she was paying rent. They couldn't believe a son would charge a mother rent. Of course they didn't know the other facts, and my mother didn't offer them. This set off a series of conversations, and my mother asked the "girls" if they knew any other people who rented within the complex. The program for the next few weeks was to talk to the renters and find out how much they were paying for rent. As I said earlier, property in Florida was hot, and the owners were getting large rentals for their properties, fortunately, significantly higher than the amount my mother was paying me. Thankfully, this subject was put to bed.

My mother established a daily routine which included walking to the grocery store every day. She liked to cook fresh vegetables, and would purchase them every day. She did this rain or shine, and even though neighbors would offer her a ride she refused, even when it was raining. The "girls" told my mother that the bank always had fresh coffee and cookies in the lobby for their customer's convenience. The bank was next to the grocery store, so this was added to her daily ritual.

I had made arrangements for her social security check to be direct deposited to her checking account. She didn't like that arrangement, even after I explained that it was safer and the money would be available quicker. She smiled and said it was OK. The banker told me that she came in every month to draw out the money, including the cents. "[So much for that.]"

After lunch, she would spend the afternoons by the pool doing her exercises in the water. She would then join in the conversation that took place. She stayed in most evenings, watching TV or playing cards by herself. When there were activities in the theater building, she would always buy tickets and attend the events. Some evenings they would gather around the pool, light the torches, listen to music and dance. She never missed that activity because she loved music and dancing. The "girls" belonged to the choral group and invited mother to join them.

She agreed, even though she had a terrible voice. The group would travel to other senior sites, including nursing homes, to entertain. My mother really enjoyed this as it gave her an opportunity to be with her friends and always included a free lunch. Most of the people in the group were much younger than my mother. She asked Yvonne not to mention her age, as she was afraid that they might exclude her from this activity. The truth of the matter was that mother was livelier than most of the younger members.

Every Saturday she would go the beauty salon to have her hair done. She was a vain person and wanted to always look nice. In fact, she always was dressed to the hilt wearing earrings, a pearl necklace and at least one bracelet. She now became an active member of Hadassah again, and attended all of their meetings and luncheons. She watched the "girls" playing bridge in the afternoons, but they never invited her to participate. There was a clique of eight who played together all the time, switching tables between themselves and no one else. This bothered her, but she never said anything to the "girls", as she didn't want to stir up the pot or ruin their friendship. What she did do was to tear out all of the bridge games printed in the newspaper and played the game by herself.

Mother was very active during the first few years she was there. She was enjoying herself, happy to keep her independence and was constantly busy. The joke of the matter was that she would not admit that to me, because in the back of her mind she felt that I rushed her into this situation. As the years progressed, you could see that she was slowing down and participating less in activities. I had to take over the payments for some of her monthly expenses. The bill that raised the most suspicion was from her pharmacy. It was over $150.00 every month. I decided to contact the pharmacy to find out about the medicine she was taking. The pharmacist laughed when I talked to him as he told me the story. Mother's basic medicines cost around $50.00. The other $100.00 was for two tubes of Retin A, a wrinkle cream. He tried to discourage her from purchasing the cream, as he knew she was in her early 90s. She told him that if she didn't get the cream she would go to another pharmacy for her pills. The next time I spoke with Mother, I mentioned that the cost of the cream was around $100, as she had no idea what her pharmacy bill was. She, being frugal, told me that she would no longer purchase it as it didn't work anyways.

She loved company, and was happy when Yvonne or I would come to visit. We spoke to her frequently during the week to make sure everything was going fine. She always asked about our family, and was anxious to know how the grandchildren were doing. When we asked how she was doing, she never admitted that she was happy to be in Florida but did admit sometimes that she got lonely and missed us. We told her that we would try to visit her more frequently, and when she got that lonely feeling to pick up the phone and call. Our daughter was in college in Boston, and when we told her about her grandmother getting lonely, she asked if she could go visit with her during spring break and bring her roommate with her. I told her it was fine with me, but she had to clear it with my mother. Needless to say my mother was thrilled that her granddaughter wanted to see her, and was looking forward to meeting her friend.

Our daughter's roommate lived in Jacksonville, Florida and they flew there first to see her parents. They spent most of the time there, but they had 4 days left to spend with my mother in Plantation; a suburb of Ft. Lauderdale. Spring break in Ft. Lauderdale was famous worldwide, and our daughter and friend wanted to participate in the experience at least one evening. They asked my mother if they could go to spend Friday night at the beach in nearby Ft. Lauderdale. She told them that she was responsible for their safety, and the only way she would allow them to go is if she came with them. Picture this if you can. Two young college students walking into a packed bar with my five foot 85 year old mother. My daughter said that everyone looked surprised, opened a path for them to get to the bar, and a young man got up to give my mother his bar stool. My mother, who does not drink, was the center of attention, leaving my daughter and friend alone to mingle and socialize with the guys at the bar. When they got home, my mother told them that she had a good time and hoped they would come back next year so they could do it again. The rest of the time there, the young girls hung around the pool wearing their bikinis trying to get a tan while the proud grandmother introduced them to everyone.

The next five years were uneventful, with the exception of one incident. My mother collected and loved candle holders. At Christmas time, my partner sent her a package which contained four candle holders which when lined in a row spelled NOEL. My mother loved the gift, told me to thank my partner, and asked who was LEON. Apparently, she must have spent some time juggling the candle holders until she arrived at Leon.

My mother continued to travel north to attend all family events up to age 95. She never missed a birthday, graduation, wedding, birth or anniversary. She loved to display her US Air assistance pin, provided to her while traveling, and was pleased at the special treatment she got. As a matter of fact, she had quite a collection probably hoping they would be worth something some day.

We tried to come to Florida more frequently, as we realized that she was becoming more frail and forgetful. She refused to allow us to get her some help, even though I think my mother realized she was having problems. I tried to get her to wear a lifeline necklace in case of an emergency. She refused, telling me that she would probably need to call 911 while she slipped in the shower, and she wasn't going to be carried out naked. Yvonne was spending weeks at a time in Florida to evaluate the situation. She was unable to convince her to get help. My mother was adamant and stubborn.

The day after Yvonne got home, we got a call that my mother had fallen and had broken her hip. Yvonne rushed back to Florida to stay with her throughout her recovery period. I came back and forth on weekends, as I was still working full time. This was the beginning of the challenge period. My mother was trying to be independent and still had a mean stubborn streak. After the hospital stay for her broken hip, they put her in a rehab facility. The doctors told us it would take months for her to recover. She hated the place, so she asked for double and triple treatments and extra therapy. She was out in three weeks. From this point forward, she had to have household help.

Yvonne called an employment agency, and was able to find part time help. They assisted in doing grocery shopping, some light cooking and cleaning, but most importantly making sure mother took the right medicine at the right time. Each was residents of Jamaica who had green cards to work in America. They all wore white uniforms at work. For some reason this bothered my mother. We were comfortable with them, and felt lucky to have them until I got a call from an immigration officer telling me that my mother's helper's green card expired, and she hadn't renewed it. He told me that they arrested her and took her to jail. He told me I was going to be fined for hiring an illegal. I asked who did he leave to take care of my mother until we hired someone else? He told me that was my problem. Needless to say the conversation got heated, and I told him I was going to have him fired. I contacted the Plantation police department and explained that she had a valid green card when we hired her. They contacted "ICE" and cleared the fine.

Neighbors stayed with my mother until the next day, when Yvonne flew to Florida to hire someone else. She got names of several people in order to establish a backup list in case there were any more problems. We had difficulty keeping help as my mother didn't want them around. I would get to my office early in the morning, and sure enough I had a voicemail. The first one was from the aide Yvonne hired telling me she didn't know where my mother was. I couldn't believe what I was hearing. They finally found my mother in the exercise room sitting on a bike, hiding from the aide with a big smile on her face. We sent the aide packing, and hired the next name on the list. This was fine until I arrived in my office the next day, and had another voice mail on my phone. This time it was from my mother. This is what she said." Good morning Joseph. This is your mother. You know the lady Yvonne hired yesterday. Nice lady. I fired her. Have a good day." What a way to start my day.

We contacted Jewish Family Services and explained the problem we were having and asked for guidance. They suggested a woman who they had worked with on other cases, who would evaluate my mom and then hire the appropriate personnel to watch over her. The lady met mother, did the evaluation, hired the people and explained to my mother that they were the woman's employees and that mother couldn't fire them. This worked out well for the first month. The lady in charge always wore business clothes, and the aides wore the white uniforms. After the lady in charge completed her evaluation, I received a call from my mother that went like this. "Hotsy totsy was here asking a lot of dumb questions and I gave her the right answers. I hope you are not paying her too much because she is useless." That was the last thing I wanted to hear. Since we were having help for two shifts which wasn't working, perhaps we needed to get full time live-in help or bring her to Albany and put her in a long term care facility.

Yvonne and I both agreed it would be better to leave her in Florida with her friends and in the warm climate. The next day, I flew to Florida to visit with mother and to find full time care. I placed an ad in the paper and began to interview candidates. They all came to the apartment for the interview and to meet my mother. She really didn't understand what was happening, but smiled throughout the entire process. I narrowed it down and finally selected a woman named Katherine, but we called her Kathy, who I thought was perfect. She held the position of deacon in a large black congregation who seemed to have compassion and understanding. She also had two adult daughters who could assist if she needed time off. This worked out well. She did everything for my mother. She cooked, cleaned, took her for rides and stayed with her around the pool. The woman prayed during her spare time and this got Sophie's interest. They got along fantastically and Sophie was now a happy camper.

One funny story before I close this chapter. On Christmas Eve, Kathy had to be at her church and took Sophie with her as her daughters were going to be there too. The service was a typical revival program with loud minstrel music and lots of dancing. It lasted until early in the morning, and it kept Sophie's interest during the entire time. She told me she had the best time of her life.

Yvonne continued to travel to Florida to visit with mother, and was comfortable with the care that Kathy was providing for her. The residents were familiar with Yvonne because of her frequent visits. They always looked forward to her stays in Florida, as she was good company for them as well.

Several men played tennis each morning and couldn't wait for Yvonne to join their group. Each of them wanted to have Yvonne as their partner, since she was the best player among them. Yvonne enjoyed playing with them, but commented that their line calls were questionable. The men were very competitive and didn't like losing to each other. They always argued about who should provide the tennis balls and sometimes acted very childish. When Yvonne was in town, that wasn't a problem, as she always brought a new can of balls each time she played with them.

The "girls" liked to play bingo and frequently invited Yvonne to join in. There was a hidden agenda there, as they didn't like driving at night. Since Yvonne always rented a car for her visits, she was able to take them to the games. She also took them shopping to the flea markets and the major malls, but really enjoyed their company.

After two years of full time care, Sophie began to exhibit severe Alzheimer symptoms, so Kathy told us she thought it was time to bring her to Albany. Since Sophie had built up a strong trust with her, we asked that she come with Sophie for the trip.

Recently sold home

This one-bedroom/one ½-bath Polynesian Gardens furnished Bernadette O'Sullivan and Linda DeWitt,

Sophie's Condo in Florida

Choral Group

Poolside

Sophie and Granddaughter Jill

Sophie and Grandson Scott

Sophie at Bar Mitzvahs and Weddings

Sophie at College Graduations

Sophie and Granddaughter at Spring Break Visit

Sophie and Granddaughter at Spring Break Visit

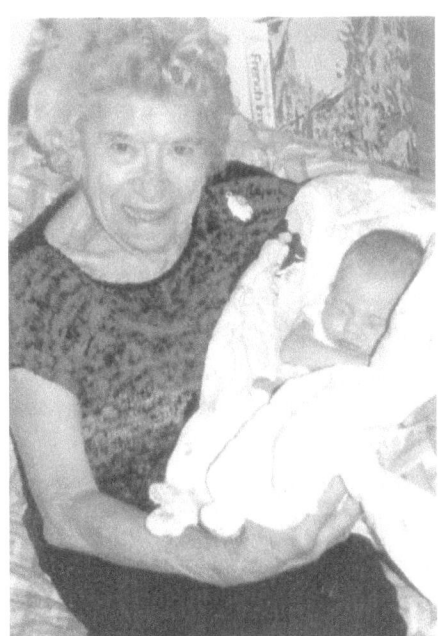

Sophie with Great-Grandchildren

ALBANY

My mother and Kathy arrived in Albany early Monday morning. Kathy was scheduled to go back to Florida on Tuesday. We contacted the long term facility, told them mother was in town, and we were ready to admit her. The facility had four separate wings, each with patients with different levels of care. The wing that they wanted to place mother in had no vacancies at the moment. They told us they could admit her and place her in another wing until a room was available in her wing. Yvonne and I discussed this and decided that it might be too much tumult for her.

Kathy asked if she could stay with mother until they admitted her to the home. She and my mother had built a strong bond of trust and affection during the two years they were together. My mother was now 98 years old and we were grateful for her request. We knew that we would experience less resistance from mother if her caregiver stayed with her. We rented a hospital bed for mother and she resided in our living room for three days until her room became available. The move to the nursing home was uneventful, and a surprise that mother didn't act up. I think she finally felt that we wanted her to be well taken care of. Kathy stayed with mother the rest of that day and left to go home the next day. We thanked her and gave her a bonus check which she truly deserved. She refused to take it at first, saying it wasn't necessary as we had compensated her adequately. We insisted. She said she would take the check, but she was going to use the money to purchase a memorial plaque in her church in memory of mother.

The transition to the home was accepted by mother, as she liked the food. It was kosher of course. I visited her every day, and on some weekends the grandkids and great-grandkids came along. She didn't say too much, but the smile she always displayed was proof that she was at peace with herself.

During 1996, while my mother was a resident of the Home, I was being honored with a prestigious award given by B'nai B'rith, as Albany Man of the Year. She was confined to a wheelchair and now spent the entire time at the home. Since all of the family came to town to attend the affair, we thought it would be appropriate to have her attend as well. There were times that she wasn't lucid, but we felt it was the right thing to do. We contracted with a Med-Vac company to transport her from the home to the facility. We were inside the facility taking pictures and meeting with the attendees when she arrived. Unknown to us, when they placed her wheelchair on the lift to remove her from the vehicle, the lift broke and she was suspended in mid air. The employees of the company panicked and the driver ran into the facility to get help to bring her down. Our two sons went outside to help remove her, and bring her into the facility. While my mother was suspended on the lift, other attendees were arriving for the event. When I spoke to them, after the event, they said that she wasn't scared or upset, and was smiling and waving to everyone and thanking them for coming to honor me.

To celebrate her 100th birthday, Yvonne arranged for the home to bake a cake large enough to feed everyone on her wing and anyone else who wanted to attend. The great-grandkids had decorated her room with hand painted pictures. The residents came to celebrate and party with her. She knew she was at the center of attention again, a place where she felt she belonged.

During the next two years, you could see mother was slowing down as she slept a lot, but she never slept through a meal. I continued to visit her daily, but it became more difficult for me because I knew that any day might be the last one. She hung in there for her 103rd birthday when four generations of our family celebrated with her. It was a beautiful day, and we were able to sit outside with her while she watched her great-grand kids playing with their toys. It was like heaven for her to be out in the fresh air and feel the wind blow in her face. Who knew how close it was to heaven? She died in her sleep a couple of months later, suffering no pain. The nurses at the home told me that it took her a long time to complete her final meal that day, but she insisted on finishing it. Thankfully, she left us without missing a meal.

Now that her journey is over, I want to end Sophie's story by saying: "Mother, we want you to know we miss you and will always love you. Thanks for the memories."

Sophie at My Award Dinner

Sophie's 100th Birthday

Sophie's 103rd Birthday

Sophie's 103rd Birthday

EULOGIES

The first eulogy was recited by Sophie's great-granddaughter Rachel Chick—Age nine at the time.

Two days ago, Sophie Simon, my great-grandmother died peacefully in her sleep. My parents told me her spirit is still here, in your heart, but that's not all that's left. Memories of all of us with her is something that will always fill up a tremendous amount of space in all our hearts, because she meant and will always mean so much to me and the rest of us: especially Poppy.

My poppy, Joseph Simon, put so much of his heart into taking care of Grandma Sophie, since she was in the Daughters of Sarah Nursing Home. If something was wrong with her, he would always be by her side. He put time away in his busy day to visit her every day.

The best memories that she left are inside my Poppy's gigantic heart. She was the best great-grandma anyone could ever have. She would make you laugh when you were sad, and she would make you laugh even if you weren't in the mood. These are only some of the things that my Grandma Sophie meant to me.

The second eulogy was recited by Sophie's great-granddaughter Tara Chick—Age eleven at the time.

We are so lucky to grow and to share all our memories with someone as kind and as sweet as Grandma Sophie. She was there when all her grandchildren and great-grand children were born. In fact, Grandma Sophie gave birth to a miracle, my grandfather, Joe Simon.

They share so many qualities, their love for each other and in fact their love for my family. Their love for us and each other is so extreme I can't tell how much I love them.

Grandma Sophie I just want to say thank you for everything you have done for my Poppy, my Mommy and Me.

The third eulogy was given by Sophie's granddaughter Sheryl Motto.

I'd like to open with a poem that reflects upon the many memories and feelings towards our grandmother on behalf of me, my husband Len and my children, Tara and Rachel.

Our Grandmother
By Susan Polis Schultz

For as long as we can remember,
you have been by our side to give us support,
to give us confidence, to give us help . . .

For as long as we can remember,
you have always been a person
we looked up to, so strong, so sensitive, so giving . . .

For as long as we can remember,
you have provided stability within the family,
full of laughter, full of tear, full of love . . .

So much of what we have become is because of you;
and we want you to know that we appreciate you,
thank you, love you and will miss you
for as long as we can remember!

For as long as we remember, Nana has been a part of our lives! From the days back in Tannersville as children, skipping stones in the creek, getting her to buy milkshakes at the restaurant next door, riding the electric horse next door, taking us ice-skating on the lake or escorting my roommate and I to a bar during Spring Break, having a better time than us because she felt responsible for us while we stayed with her!

My bat mitzvah, high school and college graduations, weddings and the birth of my children . . . her great-grandchildren . . . She was always there!

We were the lucky ones! Being local, we were able to visit her at the Nursing Home, hold her hand, feed her dinner, laugh and cry as we recalled the many stories we remembered while in her company. We were even fortunate enough to celebrate her 103rd birthday with her.

Our grandmother, Grandma Sophie as the kids called her, certainly has lived a full and happy life. For many years to come our family will continue to laugh, smile, and cry thinking about the many stories and memories that she has shared with us. Her legacy lives on.

The final eulogy was delivered by me and contains much of what is included in Sophie's memoir.

I began by saying that as I thought about the words I'd say about my mother, I realized that I need not be sad as I was very fortunate. Fortunate to have been her son!

I also said that those that knew her can recall many of the hilarious stories during her independent years in Florida. She was a remarkable woman who lived by herself for approximately fifteen years, after my father died, and until she reached age 95 when we were required to get live-in help for her.

I continued by saying that she always wanted to fend for herself, and fought for her independence until we had to bring her north to reside at the Nursing Home.

I mentioned that she was model resident, loved the food and appreciated the extraordinary care she received. I also described how she spent her final day at the home.

I concluded by telling everyone what my granddaughter, Rachel, who had wisdom beyond her years, told me the day before, at dinner, as she was trying to comfort me. "It was Grandma Sophie's time to go. She missed her husband, Jacob, and wanted to be with him."

Finally, I said that I thank G-D for the wonderful memories we have and for giving her peace without pain.

The End

Memorial Obituary

Sophie Simon, 103, died August 21, 2000 at the Daughters of Sarah Nursing Center. Mrs. Simon was born in Poland, she immigrated to the United States in 1928. Mrs. Simon lived most of her life in Tannersville, NY, where she owned and operated, with her husband the Simon's Department Store until they retired in 1977. She moved to Florida in 1980 and lived in Albany from 1995 until her death. Mrs. Simon was a life member of Hadassah and was a very active member while living in Florida. Sophie was predeceased by her husband, Jacob Simon in 1979. She is survived by her son, Joseph R. Simon and his wife, Yvonne of Loudonville; grandchildren, Mark Simon and his wife, Tracey, Sheryl Motto and her husband, Leonard and Scott Simon and his wife, Jill; great-grandchildren, Jenna, Tara, Alexa, Rachel, Kolby and Jake. Funeral services will be held Wednesday, 10 a.m. at Congregation Ohav Shalom, New Krumkill Road, Albany, NY. Interment will follow at the Kol Yisroyal Anshai Cemetery in the town of Jewett, outside Hunter, NY. The Period of Mourning will be observed at the home of Joseph and Yvonne, 21 Joy Drive, Loudonville, NY through midday Friday. Evening services will be held at the Simon residence Wednesday and Thursday at 7 p.m.

Maps

Tannersville
— Village —

Location within the state of New York

Coordinates: 42°11′37″N 74°8′20″W

Country	United States
State	New York
County	Greene

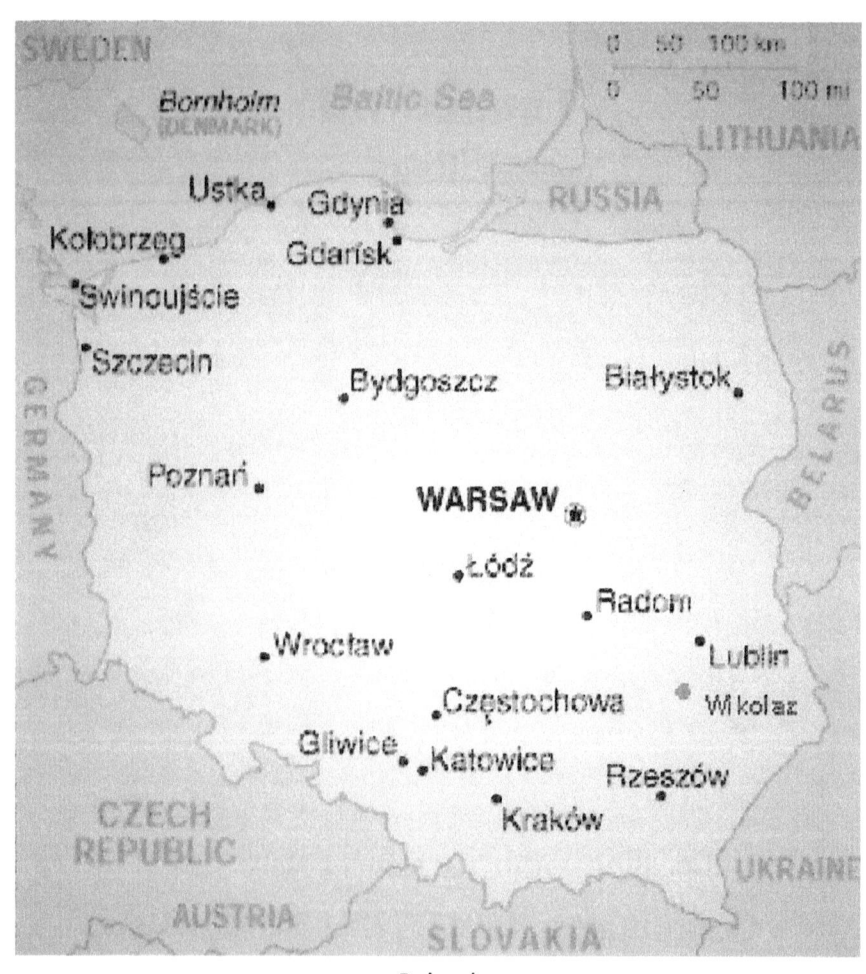

Poland

Gliniany
— Village —

Gliniany

Coordinates: 50°55′41″N 21°37′49″E

Glossary

Ballaboosteh: Typical Jewish Grandmother that always is in charge.

Bar Mitzvah: Religious service for 13 year old boys confirming their adulthood.

Bris: Circumcision ceremony when boys are 7 days old.

Bubbies: Typical Jewish Grandmother who can't do enough for you.

Challah: Braided egg bread for the Sabbath, in Yiddish.

ICE: Immigration and Customs Enforcement

Fleisich: Meat dinner meal in Yiddish.

Milkich: Dairy meal in Yiddish.

Shiva: Family of the deceased sit in mourning for a period of time.

Yiddish: The Jewish language, derived from German and written in Hebrew letters.

Epilogue

As I thought about writing the story of mother I didn't realize how much fun it would be. I knew that I was fortunate to have been her son. I also knew that our entire family was fortunate because not only was she a wonderful, loving mother, but she was a tremendously caring grandmother and an unbelievable great-grandmother.

Some Jewish grandmothers are known as "Bubbies", but my mother was known as the "Ballaboosteh" of our family. In English that translates to the Simon matriarch. She liked being at the center of all activities and loved being with her family. She attended all family functions until age 95, flying back and forth from Florida, on her own, proudly wearing her US Air assistance button. The button was provided to her so that the attendants knew that she was going to need a wheelchair and would be escorted by them to meet a family member. She never forgot anyone's birthday or anniversary, and loved celebrating her own as well. On May 13, 2000, four generations of our family celebrated her 103rd birthday. It was obvious that she was pleased that we were there as she laughed when she watched the great-grandkids running around.

My mother came to America as a teenager with just the clothes on her back and very little money in her pocketbook. It is a credit to this country's free enterprise system that a Polish immigrant could arrive in America without money, start a new life and run a successful retail store with ten years of formal education. She was street smart, had a strong work ethic, a great strength of character and was incredibly independent. She taught me to be respectful of others and to provide assistance to those in need. I'm glad that I inherited her work ethic, and I hope that I also have her longevity genes. I close with my mother's own words taken from her memoirs. "So that's what life is all about. Memories and memories. That's what makes a great life".